ERSTE ENGLISCHE WÖRTER

Lee Davis

DK
DORLING KINDERSLEY

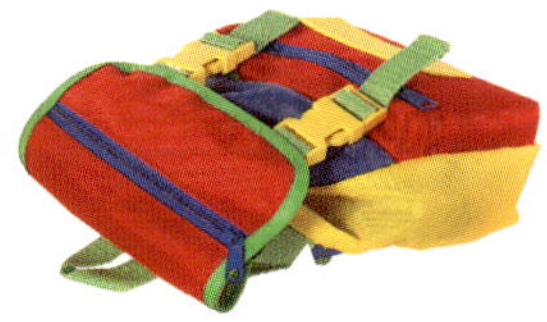

Liebe Eltern und Erzieher!

Sie halten ein beliebtes Kinderbuch in Händen, das als Einstieg in die englische Sprache bestens geeignet ist. Es wendet sich an die Vorschule und den frühbeginnenden Fremdsprachenunterricht in der Grundschule, kann aber auch zu Hause mit großem Gewinn benutzt werden.

Betrachten Sie mit den Kindern die große Abbildung in der Mitte und lesen Sie ihnen die kleine Episode vor. Dann fragen Sie die Kinder, was sie verstanden haben. Sprechen Sie ihnen nun einzelne Wörter vor, nach Möglichkeit mehrmals, und lassen Sie die Kinder nachsprechen. Im Anhang finden Sie eine englisch-deutsche Wörterliste mit der jeweiligen Aussprache der Wörter. Sind die Begriffe den Kindern vertraut, können Sie ihnen kleine Suchaufgaben stellen. Fragen Sie zum Beispiel »Where is the snail« und lassen Sie die Kinder auf die entsprechende Abbildung zeigen.

Begleiten Sie und die Kinder Teddy nun auf seiner kleinen Ballonreise.
Viel Spaß und Erfolg dabei wünscht Ihnen

Wolfgang Hamm
Fachberater Englisch für Grundschulen

TEDDY'S DAY

slippers

dressing gown

trousers

shirt

cap

pyjamas

shorts

jeans

sandals

"This is going to be a very busy day," says Teddy one morning. "What shall I wear?"

wardrobe

chest of drawers

socks

handkerchief

pants

waistcoat

scarf

hat

shoes

jumper

Can you point to some of Teddy's clothes that are

yellow   blue   red   green?

dungarees

T-shirt

rainhat

boots

school bag

purse

zip

umbrella

raincoat

sponge

soap dish

soap

hairbrush

beaker

water

mirror

seahorse

bubble bath

"I have an idea for an adventure," says Teddy. "But I've got a lot to do first!" Teddy washes his face and brushes his teeth. "Now I'm ready to start my busy day!" he says.

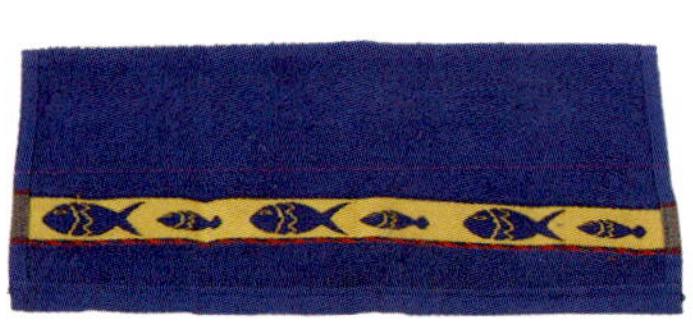
towel

bath

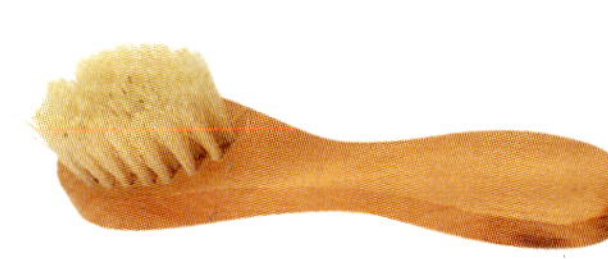
back brush

taps

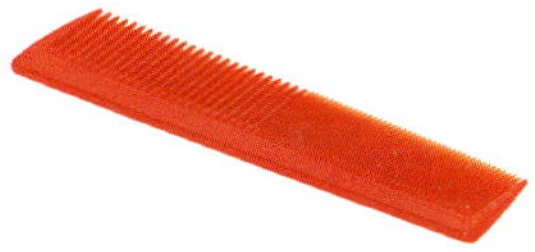
comb

flannel

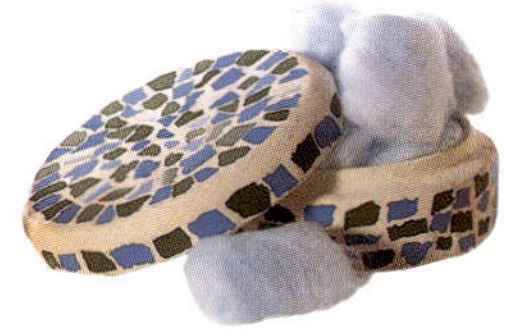
cotton wool

rubber duck

- How many bears can you see in Teddy's bathroom?
- How many brushes can you see?

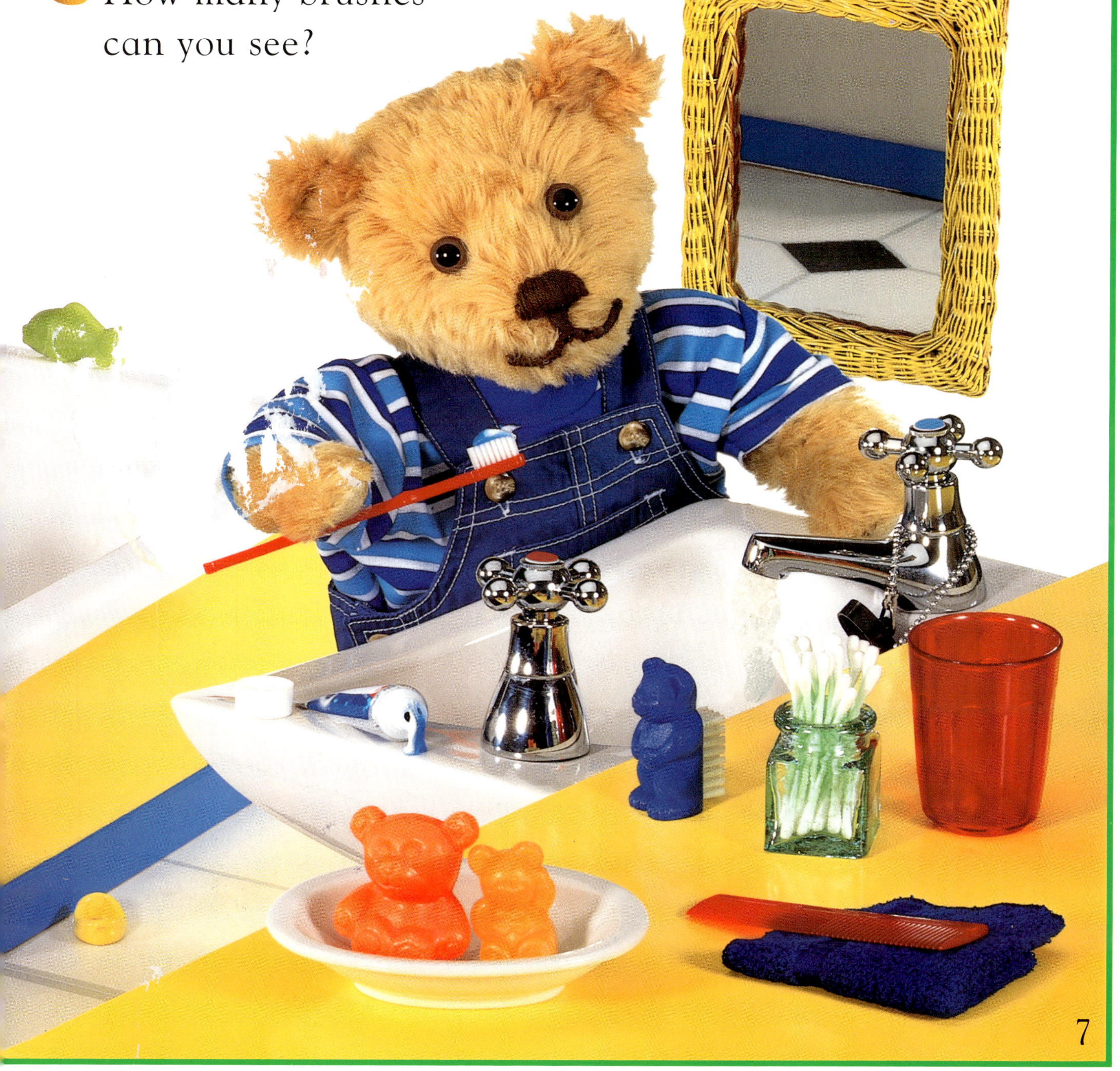

nail brush

plug

tissues

shampoo

basin

toothbrush

toothpaste

cotton buds

sofa

table

cushions

marbles

“I’m making something special,” says Teddy. “Do you know what it is? It will fly, but it’s not an aeroplane!”

- What can you see that makes music?
- What can you see that swims?

lamp

clock

toy boat

drawing

paint

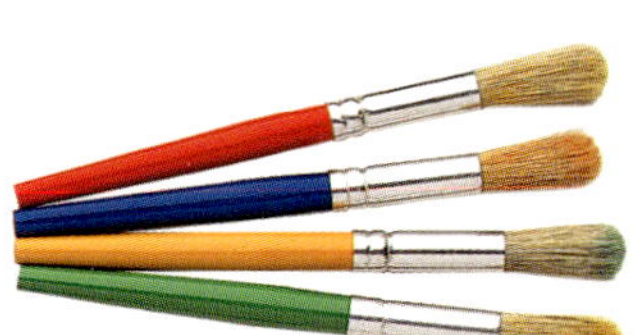
paint brushes

scissors

crayons

toy car

playing cards

jigsaw puzzle

drum

horn

blocks

basket

coloured pencils

ball

toy mouse

balloon

watering can

basket

daffodils

butterflies

caterpillar

garden rake

trowel

broom

garden fork

Teddy has made a hot-air balloon. “Ready for take off,” he says. “Goodbye, garden!”

flowerpot

seeds

clippers

fence

snail

ant

potatoes

lettuces

bean plants

Can you find…
1 bird
2 butterflies
3 lettuces
4 daffodils
5 ants?

carrots

tomatoes

tree

bird

hot-air balloon

grass

binoculars

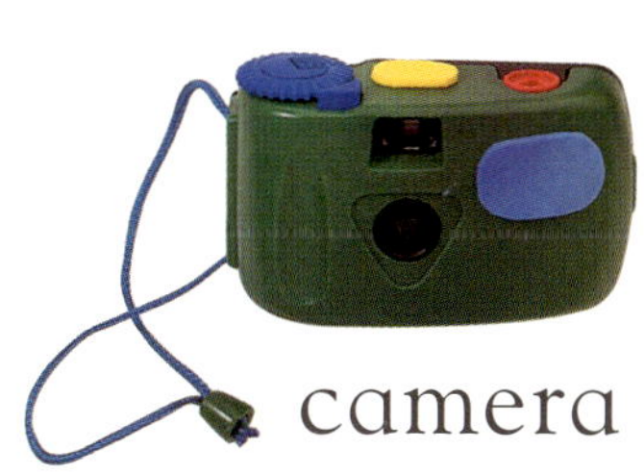
camera

tent

fence

cloud

mountains

well

windmill

tractor

caravan

farmhouse

barn

bridge

train

village

rabbit

ducklings

duck

cow

The balloon is flying above the countryside.
The animals on the ground look very small.
Do you know …

- which animal is standing on the bridge?
- which animal is standing on the fence?

goose

pig

sheep

cockerel

cat

horse

frog

bird

chicken

hat

sunglasses

towel

postcards

pencil

sun block

sandwich

Bob

Roscoe

The balloon flies to the seaside
and lands on the beach.
“Ahoy!” Teddy calls out to
some friends.

Dermott

fish

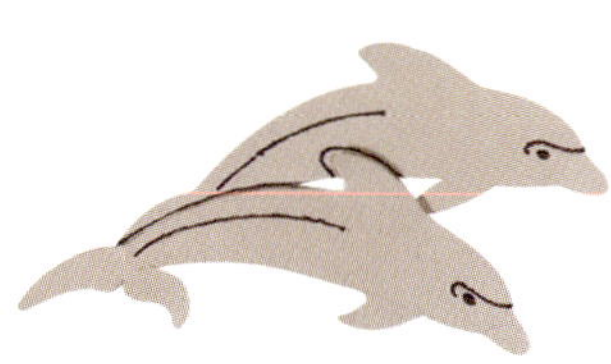

dolphins

starfish

sea

pebbles

rock

seagull

Can you find these shapes at the seaside?

circle   star   rectangle

square   triangle

lighthouse

boat

sandcastle

spade

sand

seaweed

shells

bucket

waiter

bicycle

aeroplane

bus

Soon, the balloon is flying over a street. Teddy looks down on the offices and restaurants, the hospital and the cinema. "What a busy town!" he says.

policeman

nurse

fireman

office worker

chair

table

cinema

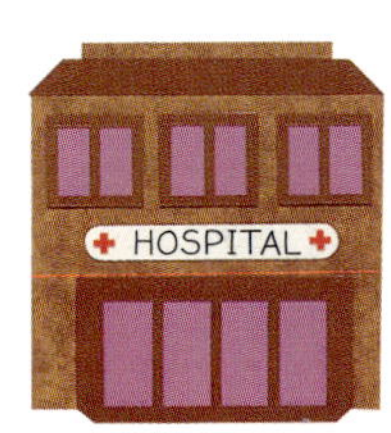

hospital

car

motorcycle

fire engine

postman

How many nurses can you see?
How many waiters can you see?
How many firemen can you see?

letter box

road sign

traffic light

restaurant

supermarket

café

office block

flower seller

sun

pond

bee

grasshopper

trees

tree house

bench

slide

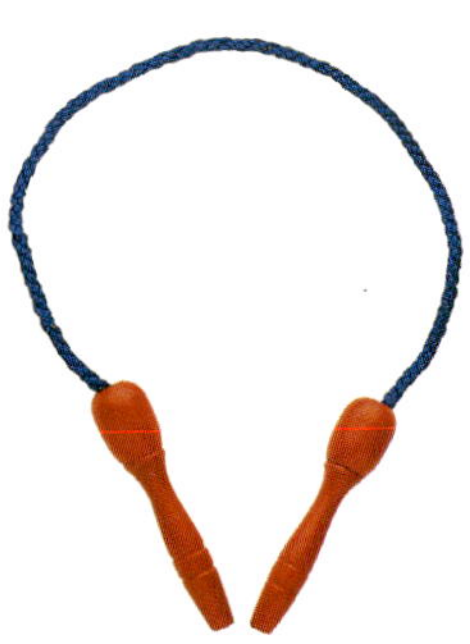
skipping rope

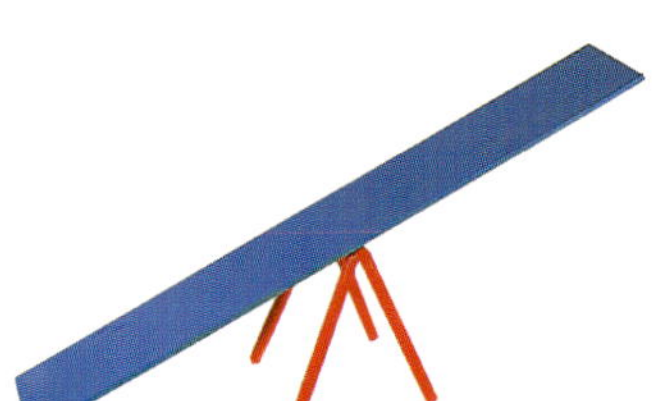
seesaw

swing

skateboard

ladybird

lunch box

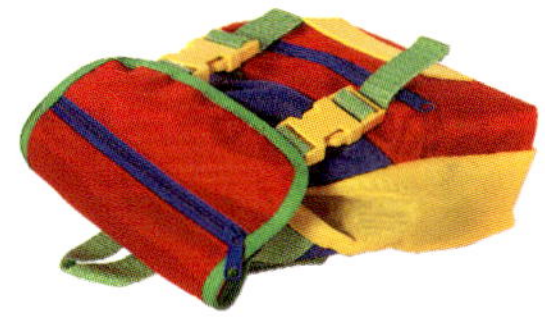

rucksack

Florrie

Then Teddy sees some friends in the playground.
"Stop and play with us," they call.
"Sorry, I can't!" says Teddy.
"It's time for dinner!"

Dixie

Hilda

Milly

Russell

ball

bats

hoop

orange juice

butter

bowl

carrots

celery

honey

bread

ice cream

plates

Teddy is back at home. “All that travelling has made me hungry!” he says.

mugs

salt and pepper

washing-up liquid

cupboard

breadsticks

grapes

apple

lemon

cereal

Look at the things to eat in Teddy's kitchen.

- Which are hot? Which are cold?
- Which are sweet? Which are sour?
- Which are hard? Which are soft?

spaghetti

toaster

brush

dustpan

knife

fork

spoon

kettle

saucepan

cooker

table

rug

torch

friends

lamp

clock

notebook

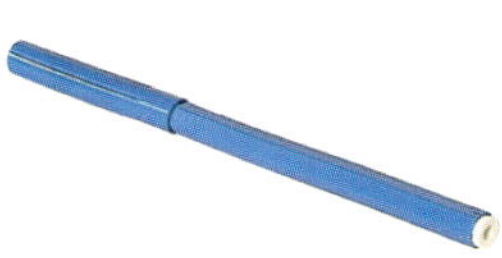

pen

diary

shoes

binoculars

slippers

photographs

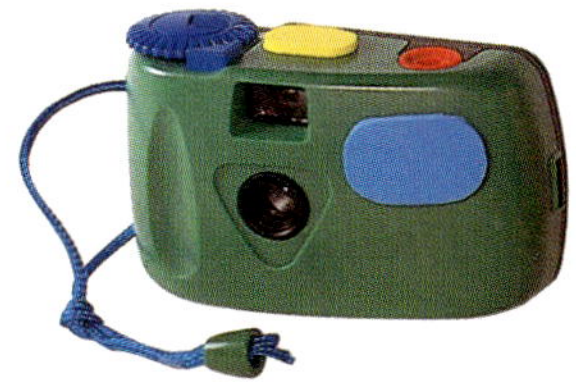

camera

telescope

vase

"It **has** been a busy day and now I'm very sleepy," says Teddy.
"Good night."

What do you see through Teddy's window?

daffodils

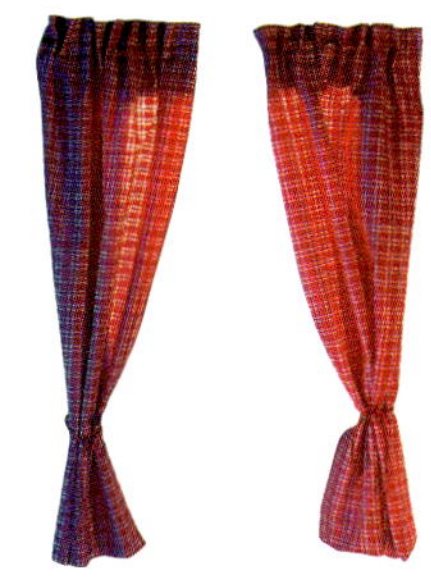

curtains

moon

window

book

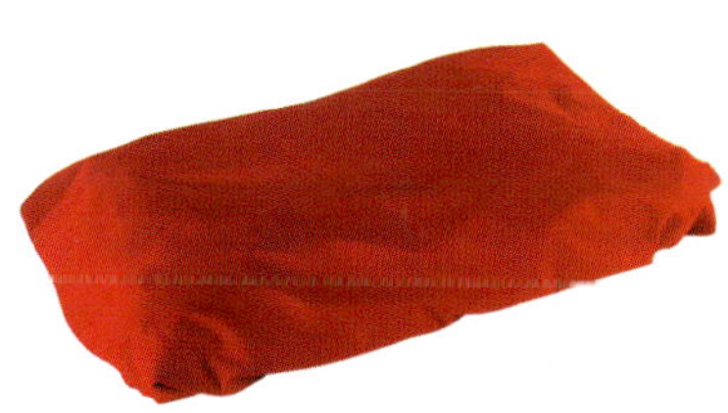

duvet

stars

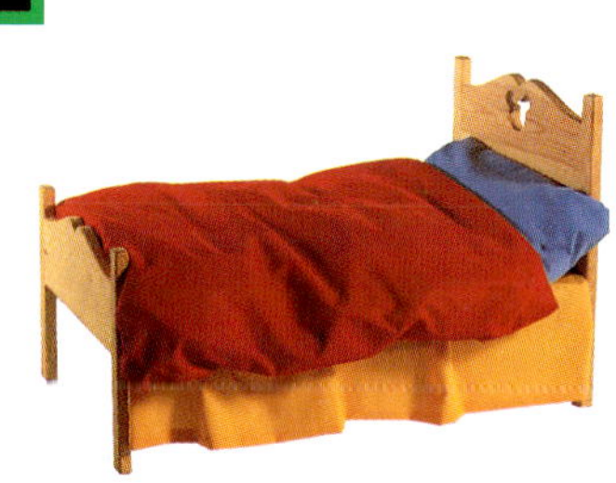

bed

Englisch		Deutsch
A		
aeroplane	[ˈeərəpleɪn]	Flugzeug
ant	[ænt]	Ameise
apple	[ˈæpl]	Apfel
B		
back brush	[ˈbækˌbrʌʃ]	Rückenbürste
ball	[bɔːl]	Ball
balloon	[bəˈluːn]	Ballon
barn	[baːn]	Scheune
basin	[ˈbeɪsn]	Waschbecken
basket	[ˈbaːskɪt]	Korb
bath	[baːθ]	Badewanne
bats	[bæts]	Schläger
beaker	[ˈbiːkə]	Zahnputzbecher
bean plants	[biːn plaːnts]	Bohnenpflanzen
bed	[bed]	Bett
bee	[biː]	Biene
bench	[bentʃ]	Bank
bicycle	[ˈbaɪsɪkl]	Fahrrad
binoculars	[biˈnɒkjʊləz]	Fernglas
bird	[bɜːd]	Vogel
blocks	[blɒks]	Bauklötze
blue	[bluː]	Blau
boat	[bəʊt]	Boot
book	[bʊk]	Buch
boots	[buːts]	(Gummi-)Stiefel
bowl	[bəʊl]	Schüssel
bread	[bred]	Brot
breadsticks	[ˈbredstiks]	Brotstangen
bridge	[brɪdʒ]	Brücke
broom	[bruːm]	Besen
brush	[brʌʃ]	Handfeger
bubble bath	[ˈbʌblˌbaːθ]	Schaumbad
bucket	[ˈbʌkɪt]	Eimer
bus	[bʌs]	Bus
butter	[ˈbʌtə]	Butter
butterflies	[ˈbʌtəflaɪz]	Schmetterlinge
C		
café	[ˈkæfeɪ]	Café
camera	[ˈkæmərə]	Kamera
cap	[kæp]	Schirmmütze
car	[kaː]	Auto
caravan	[ˈkærəvæn]	Wohnwagen
carrots	[ˈkærəts]	Karotten
cat	[kæt]	Katze
caterpillar	[ˈkætəpɪlə]	Raupe
celery	[ˈseləri]	Sellerie
cereal	[ˈsɪərɪəl]	Getreideflocken
chair	[tʃeə]	Stuhl
chest of drawers	[tʃest əv drɔːz]	Kommode
chicken	[ˈtʃɪkɪn]	Huhn
cinema	[ˈsɪnəmə]	Kino
circle	[ˈsɜːkl]	Kreis
clippers	[ˈklipəz]	Heckenschere
clock	[klɒk]	Uhr

cloud	[klaʊd]	Wolke
cockerel	['kɒkərəl]	Hahn
coloured pencils	['kʌləd 'penslz]	Buntstifte
comb	[kəʊm]	Kamm
cooker	['kʊkə]	Herd
cotton buds	['kɒtn,bʌdz]	Wattestäbchen
cotton wool	['kɒtn,wʊl]	Watte
cow	[kaʊ]	Kuh
crayons	['kreɪənz]	Wachsmalstifte
cupboard	['kʌbəd]	Schrank
curtains	['kɜːtnz]	Vorhänge
cushions	['kʊʃnz]	Kissen

D

daffodils	['dæfədɪlz]	Osterglocken
diary	['daɪərɪ]	Tagebuch
dolphins	['dɒlfɪnz]	Delfine
drawing	['drɔːɪŋ]	Zeichnung
dressing gown	['dresɪŋ,gaʊn]	Bademantel
drum	[drʌm]	Trommel
duck	[dʌk]	Ente
ducklings	['dʌklɪŋz]	Entenküken
dungarees	[,dʌŋgə'rɪːz]	Latzhose
dustpan	['dʌstpæn]	Handschaufel
duvet	['duːveɪ]	Bettdecke

F

farmhouse	['faːmhaʊs]	Bauernhaus
fence	[fens]	Zaun
fire engine	['faɪərendʒɪn]	Feuerwehrauto
fireman	['faiəmən]	Feuerwehrmann
fish	[fɪʃ]	Fische
flannel	['flænl]	Waschlappen
flower seller	['flaʊəselə]	Blumenverkäufer
flowerpot	['flaʊəpɒt]	Blumentopf
fork	[fɔːk]	Gabel
friends	[frendz]	Freunde
frog	[frɒg]	Frosch

G

garden fork	['gaːdn,fɔːk]	Gartengabel
garden rake	['gaːdn,reɪk]	Harke
goose	[guːs]	Gans
grapes	[greɪps]	Weintrauben
grass	[graːs]	Gras
grasshopper	['graːs,hɒpə]	Grashüpfer
green	[griːn]	Grün

H

hairbrush	['heə,brʌʃ]	Haarbürste
handkerchief	['hæŋkətʃɪf]	Taschentuch
hat	[hæt]	Hut
honey	['hʌnɪ]	Honig
hoop	[huːp]	Reifen
horn	[hɔːn]	Tröte
horse	[hɔːs]	Pferd
hospital	['hɒspɪtl]	Krankenhaus
hot-air balloon	[hɒt'eə bə'luːn]	Heißluftballon

I–J

ice cream	['aɪskriːm]	Eis
jeans	[dʒiːnz]	Jeans
jigsaw puzzle	['dʒɪgsɔː,pʌzl]	Puzzle
jumper	['dʒʌmpə]	Pullover

K–L

kettle	['ketl]	Wasserkessel
knife	[naɪf]	Messer
ladybird	['leɪdɪbɜːd]	Marienkäfer
lamp	[læmp]	Lampe

lemon	['lemən]	Zitrone
letter box	['letəbɒks]	Briefkasten
lettuces	['letɪsɪz]	Salatköpfe
lighthouse	['laithaʊs]	Leuchtturm
lunch box	['lʌntʃbɒks]	Brotdose

M–N

marbles	['maːblz]	Murmeln
mirror	['mɪrə]	Spiegel
moon	[muːn]	Mond
motorcycle	['məʊtəˌsaikl]	Motorrad
mountains	['maʊntɪnz]	Berge
mugs	[mʌgz]	Tassen
nail brush	['neilˌbrʌʃ]	Nagelbürste
notebook	['nəʊtbʊk]	Notizbuch
nurse	[nɜːs]	Krankenschwester

O–P

office block	['ɒfis blɒk]	Bürogebäude
office worker	['ɒfis 'wɜːkə]	Büroangestellter
orange juice	['ɒrɪndʒdʒuːs]	Orangensaft
paint	[peɪnt]	Farbe
paint brushes	['peɪntˌbrʌʃɪz]	Pinsel
pants	[pænts]	Unterhose
pebbles	['peblz]	Kieselsteine
pen	[pen]	Stift
pencil	['pensl]	Bleistift
photographs	['fəʊtəgraːfs]	Fotos
pig	[pɪg]	Schwein
plates	[pleɪts]	Teller
playing cards	['pleɪɪŋkaːdz]	Spielkarten
plug	[plʌg]	Stöpsel
policeman	[pə'liːsmən]	Polizist
pond	[pɒnd]	Teich
postcards	['pəʊstkaːdz]	Postkarten
postman	['pəʊstmən]	Postbote
potatoes	[pə'teɪtəʊz]	Kartoffeln
purse	[pɜːs]	Geldbeutel
pyjamas	[pə'dʒaːməz]	Schlafanzug

R

rabbit	['ræbɪt]	Kaninchen
raincoat	['reɪnkəʊt]	Regenmantel
rainhat	['reɪnhæt]	Regenhut
rectangle	['rektæŋgl]	Rechteck
red	[red]	Rot
restaurant	['restərɒnt]	Restaurant
road sign	['rəʊdsaɪn]	Straßenschild
rock	[rɒk]	Stein
rubber duck	['rʌbə dʌk]	Quietsche-Entchen
rucksack	['rʌksæk]	Rucksack
rug	[rʌg]	Teppich

S

salt and pepper	['sɔːltn'pepə]	Salz und Pfeffer
sand	[sænd]	Sand
sandals	['sændlz]	Sandalen
sandcastle	['sændkaːsl]	Sandburg
sandwich	['sænwɪdʒ]	Sandwich
saucepan	['sɔːspən]	Kochtopf
scarf	[skaːf]	Schal
school bag	['skuːlbæg]	Schultasche
scissors	['sɪzəz]	Schere
sea	[siː]	Meer
seagull	['siːgʌl]	Möwe
seahorse	['siːhɔːs]	Seepferdchen
seaweed	['siːwiːd]	Seetang
seeds	[siːdz]	Samen
seesaw	['siːsɔː]	Wippe
shampoo	[ʃæm'puː]	Haarshampoo